Pl
Fl
M

MW00779432

"A delicate blend of ecological awareness and mythological sensibility, *Field Guide to Invasive Species of Minnesota* lures the reader in with a semblance of clarity and rationality, and then tips you into a complex surreal world that resembles ours—it is ours—but is also not. I want to wrestle with some of these poems until they yield meaning, but they dance, just out of reach, evanescent and tantalizing."

—Deborah L. Davitt, author of *The Gates of Never*

"A thoughtful and intelligent collection of one-page poems and elegant illustrations that slowly bud from gentle cricket song into a poison-leafed and weedy future. Field Guide to Invasive Species of Minnesota is a thorned and exciting imagining where each specimen is handled as if by a daring and sun-smeared trickster, the delight in getting muddy and making up stories proudly prominent, and a refreshing pleasure in a collection of nature poetry."

—Julie Reeser, author of *Beak, Full of Tongue* and *Terracotta Pomegranate*

"This good book by Amelia Gorman really struck a nerve. Minnesota was my happy summer home for decades. Then some hideous things called Zebra Mussels showed up in the water and somehow seemed to ruin everything. It never occurred to me to write a dystopian book about the horror and alienation these things caused. I wish I had. This is a clever and enjoyable chapbook that captures the mood of how our lives are invaded by change."

—John Philip Johnson, Pushcart Prize-winning science fiction writer and poet

"Poems inspired by ecological destruction—both ongoing and potential—can be difficult to pull off. But Amelia Gorman has triumphantly managed it here, turning to 21 different invasive species as springs for 21 different poems, ranging from short brutal lyrics to more complicated prose poems. Leaping between the now and near-future, they offer warning and hope in near measure, with lovely and shocking images. If you've never connected mute swans and pianos before now, nor contemplated the full meaning of your desire for an unblocked view - well, you will after this. A timely and needed collection, especially recommended for readers interested in poems that straddle the lines between the literary and the speculative."

—Mari Ness, author of *Through Immortal Shadows Singing* and *Resistance and Transformation: On Fairy Tales*.

Field Guide to Invasive Species of Minnesota

AMELIA GORMAN

INTERSTELLAR FLIGHT PRESS

This is a work of fiction. All of the characters, organizations, and events portrayed are either products of the author's imagination or used fictitiously.

FIELD GUIDE TO INVASIVE SPECIES OF MINNESOTA

Text Copyright © 2021 by Amelia Gorman

Edited by Holly Lyn Walrath.

Published by Interstellar Flight Press
Houston, Texas.
www.interstellarflightpress.com

ISBN (eBook): 978-1-953736-03-1
ISBN (Paperback): 978-1953736-01-7

First Edition: 2020

TABLE OF CONTENTS:

No.1. — Brittle
Naiad

Brittle Naiad

Brittle as the snow is gray,
she has secrets for one who will listen
We all miss the old world.

Being can count as an action
at four meters fathomed, she whispers
There is nothing safe about houses.

Submersed sybil of the Mississippi,
one day a year she rises, saying
Harvesting is hard for roots unwoven.

Oracle, nautical,
tells the traveler in noxious tones
Men drown when you choke their machines.

Boats beach themselves
in the storms on her winter shores
Sinking is its own reward,

Ice ghosts
decay along the floes
And breaking is its own survival strategy.

No. 2. — BUCKTHORN

Buckthorn

There is no catching the fruits that
shivered, quivered, and rivered inside you.
There is no eating back the bush—
not with the help of goats or swine,
not fried into buckthorn flour pancakes.

There is only you
reckoning sand,
counting the replicating drupes
until the numbers get too large.
Forcing your way
through the ecophagic wood
as it slavers, quavers, and slivers
inside you.

And soon there will be no you.
Just endless, reproducing
thorns.

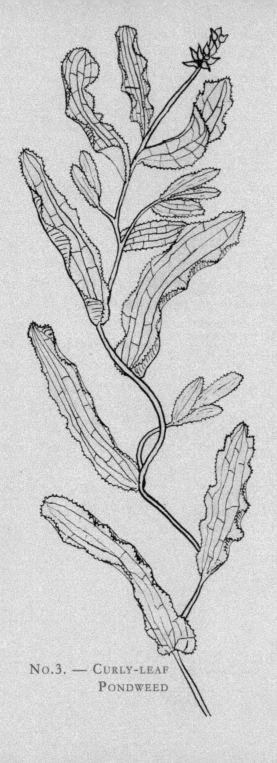

No. 3. — Curly-leaf
Pondweed

Curly-leaf Pondweed

The meltwater came
in waves and walls
until the wood barriers rotted
and the metal rusted.

So we grew new dams,
living, green, and knotted
with botanic teeth to gnash
back the water, crusted

with barnacles and wire
to build up the frame
maintaining itself high
as the water. We trusted

the truce would stay the same—
never thought the two plotted without us.

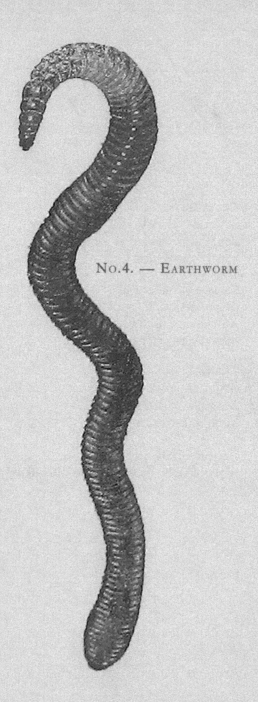

No. 4. — Earthworm

Earthworm

While cities crumble, we clasp
cast to cast, enough of us even
in them to come up worms

million mother, vertical father.

Dumped as so much half-bait
into brown lakes, algae-stained
by motors who had no faith
in our resurrection

dropped in water, in soil,
in swamp and concrete, underneath
the collapse we entwine

below the yellow air and lead
we filter yesterday's filth,
squeezing out our statues
and bringing them to life

demi-sister, half-brother
sculptor mother, dirt father.

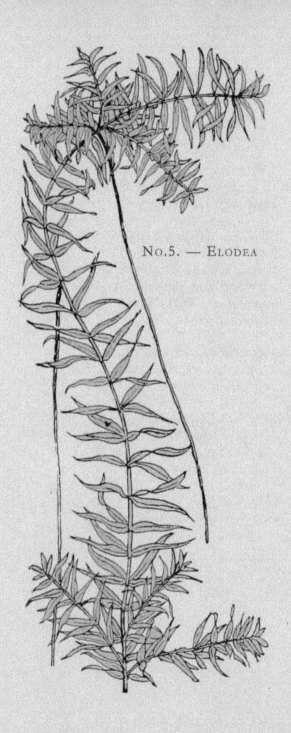

No.5. — Elodea

Elodea

In the future you can choose any death
as long as it's by water.
Execution by current's column
or a drawdown, free-floating
or else tethered.

The executioner's melody
is white with a yellow line
running through it,

a song that smells like its color,
like phosphor and eggs and sunlight.

Elodea knows where all the bodies are:
clinging to her.

Like the hangman from a fairytale
(the kind damned to live alone at the gallows),
she grows up here without a choice in the
world.

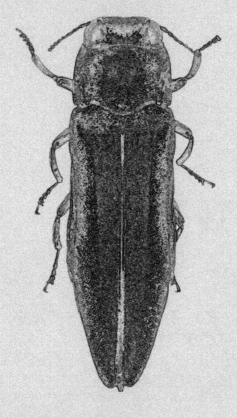

No. 6 — EMERALD ASH
BORER

Emerald Ash Borer

You always wanted a necklace
that scuttled across your skin.

You always wanted a currency
that came back to you.

You always wanted a horizon view
that stretched to the Rockies.

You always wanted the end of the world.

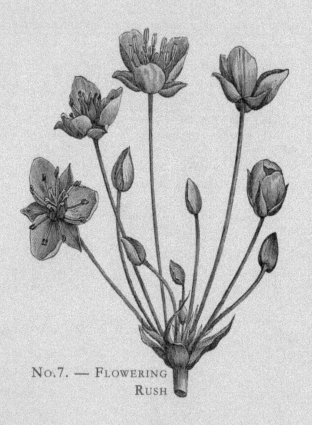

No.7. — Flowering
Rush

Flowering Rush

Hidden among the cattails and the willows,
it came here to keep to itself.
Spring-fed, like Forest Lake,
both curdle up from the underground.

Rushing to undress, it strips green seams
to show mauve skin
ripe with wet cells,
bursting umbrels dripping pollen
naked hunter
laying snares in its sacred spaces,

turning people into pines
to block out the sun
we'll burn to keep warm.

No.8. — Garlic
Mustard

Garlic Mustard

Erasure of Phytoliths in Pottery Reveal the Use of Spice in European Prehistoric Cuisine
Hayley Saul, Marco Madella, Anders Fischer,
Aikaterini Glykou, Sönke Hartz, Oliver E. Craig,
2013

The prehistoric record
is difficult.

Use a calculus
of potsherds
seeds and char,

transition from farming,
open a document,
control cells,
plant the taxon
in many parts of the world.

No. 9. — Grecian
Foxglove

Grecian Foxglove

What good is foxglove
now that we've removed our bodies?

We've gotten away from the grind
the gore and the rats and the crowds

the electrical storms
the exploding transformers
the rising waters

and death riding war into the mall.

In Mother Hutton Hall we digitize ourselves
subtract the charcoal lungs and the
sloughing skin

but the skipping hearts still
transfer binary, the defects
run straight through our code.

Can we save the digitalis on disc too?
Love is treatment, flowers kind,
hoaxes are the oldest medicine we know.

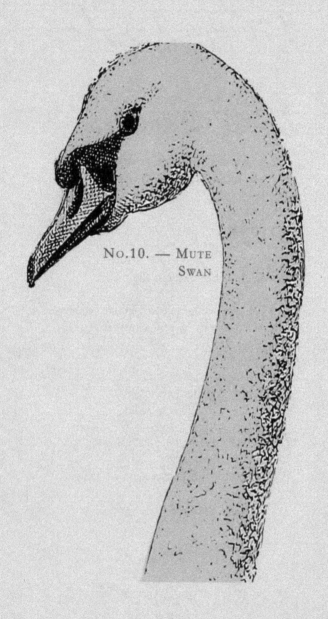

No.10. — Mute
Swan

Mute Swan

There is no fathoming these waters.
You're the cello in this piece?
I was a cello too.
Let's speak in music instead
and splash pianos on each other.

There is one fathoming of these waters
buttons sink from my shirt before a dive
when learning two things
about breaking men's legs.

There are two fathoming these waters,
then wings,
half this lake for you and
half for me
love.

No. 11. — Norway Maple

Norway Maple

How funny—
     My name is *samara*
     just like your favorite tree.

How funny—
     I grew up across the street from you
     and the paper mill,
     it closed before I could work there.

Now you and I tolerate pollution
as well as the trees
only a few tar spots on our lungs,
felt gall on our skin.

Platitudes won't kindle fires
but heartwood will after we take out the spline.

We'll tell stories about the Crimson King,
his adventures with
Schwedleri and Drummondi
and the Pendulum.

We'll learn dead hobbies like
turnery and touching.

We'll get drunk on Norway syrup all winter
it isn't sweet like the sugar maple—
no, it's something better.

No. 12. — Purple
Loosestrife

Purple loosestrife

The flowers pollinate the insects today.
Little green moths with powdery wings
photosynthesize and turn towards the sun.

Eggs grow in clusters, need to be
buried like seeds.

The vector catches the scent on
rays of the light,
goes towards the purple beacon

alights,
weighs heavy on the blossom with children,
until next summer little grubs come free,

born under the proud, sagging head of the
loosestrife.

No.13. — Queen
Anne's Lace

Queen Anne's Lace

All the meadows are frosted over.
All the prairie grasses duck and quiver,
hiding their heads in the roots.

Queen Anne's Lace tats together
its strange beauty, grafts itself up
an iron mountain, wild wedding dress.

No longer just a dot of blood,
but a whole stream pours, constant
as erosion, universal, rich as butter.

So we invent a kind of alchemy,
transfusions from the bleeding center.
Its patients grow lovage,

garlic mustard and wild onions,
pinnate leaves on their legs
ramps from their mouths and nose

carrot skin grafted on, and tiny
feathery tips of green eyelashes
better absorb the sun in a year
that will be wracked with famine
and plush with wild vegetable humans.

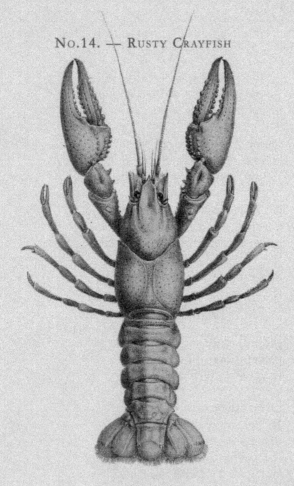

Rusty Crayfish

Beyond the border of tar and river
two claws grapple in the bladder-bracken.
Buoyant ferns crochet a matrix
over corpses shallow in the Mississippi.

For anyone with boots,
snowshoes,
the right tendril-toes,
some antique nickels,
or a can of beans,
betting is ripe on the Mississippi

where the rusty crayfish march and skitter
over fiddlehead farms and seaweed banners.

Vacuum eyes and flicking rods,
clicking claws and iron coats
oxidize in that strip of cold green
water, their mother a toxic vein
dripping into the Mississippi.

Clash of claws, of iron scars, we gamble
on which giant capsizes, which swims away
like we gamble on every sip of water,
every step on eroded ledges
when we dive for the shattered carapace
of our own secret wars.

No.15. — Sea Lamprey

Sea Lamprey

We thought when this planet was full we'd expand into space, but we became too laden with objects to make the needed change, so we edged into the water instead, pushing the wild further out to sea.

Then it wasn't strange when a lamprey that effortlessly swapped lake for sea over time found how to induce in itself another kind of liminal change and attach to the outside of our failed shuttles making for space—

our failure only, not theirs, they never returned to the sea and, detaching from our metal, they carved themselves a new space fattened on our oil, their very being began to change

their metamorphosis took them to space, ours drove us underground.

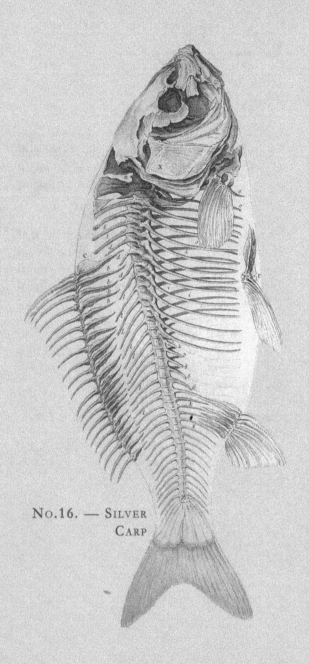

No. 16. — Silver Carp

Silver Carp

You were taught to bait a hook at three
clean a butcher block at five (never bleach)
but oil and vinegar meant
for eating.

So you learned to clean a carp at age seven
August 2nd, 2045.

Cut off the eyestalks, scrape off the snails
then you can scale it, first the outside layer,
then the inside.

Lastly, always check the stomach
for a silver coin

after your mother lost a molar
biting hard one sweaty summer night
at the dinner table.

It won't grant you a wish,
but you can keep your teeth in this world.

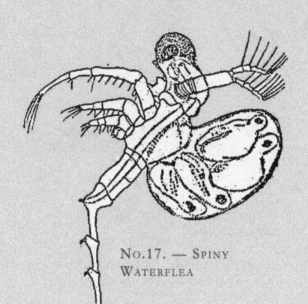

No.17. — Spiny
Waterflea

Spiny Waterflea

Act I.

The spiny water fleas enjoy a game of water polo. See their good sportsmanship as they flit about to congratulate the winners and assure the losers of their good play.

Watch as they put away their things after the game, model citizens and good Christians.

Act II.

The waterfleas are miners, they take rare elements out of the earth and sell them to the highest bidder. Look at their tiny picks and hats. Safety is important, even for a flea.

Act III.

These fleas are reenacting a great Roman circus. Behold, they race around the Circus Maximus in miniature. The winner will get a crown of the smallest stonewort flowers.

Act I.

Mlle. Cladeaux pulls into yet another dying river town, 45-liter bag on her back full of all her things. It's a cold night in Helsen Shore Minnesota.

She pulls out a flask of moonshine and prepares to go into performer mode. To go mad on the moon and river and the gully, to show up tomorrow barking and busking.

Act II.

She refashioned their little picks out of icepicks and paperclips. She hasn't seen ice in years, though she hears up north they have more than they can handle. She drinks a moonshine neat as she labors under the magnifying glass.

Act III.

Someone in the audience asks if it isn't weird that fleas are pulling other fleas in chariots. She remembers before she bought the flea circus she pulled out of the mud-sledges for tourists along the drying river beds. She bites her tongue until it bleeds.

Starry Stonewort

*Zodiac Astrological Signs of the Future as Found in
Constellations in Starry Stonewort
Horoscope for the week of Aug 13 2046*

Mycoheterotroph
> You will be hungry, but it's a familiar
> hunger. You can find pictures of food,
> if not food.

Frostbite
> The Stonewort sees a deceiving week.
> Lost days. Lost electricity and clean
> water. Watch out for the rash that
> comes from bathing it the lake, it burns
> like ice.

Erosion
> The Stonewort wishes you well but
> warns you of the worst. Huge loss is
> inevitable, you'll be lighter afterwards.

Two-headed
> Those born under the sign of the Two-
> headed should avoid the sky today.

Casino
> Drown your enemies before they drown
> you, bottle the memories of your
> friends, don't lose a single drop.

Little Fisher

> Beware of parasites and other thoughts
> that burrow too deep to remove.

Acid Rain

> The succulent stars see travel in your
> future, water flowing upriver instead of
> down.

The Gateway

> The Moon's Reflection floats through
> your sign, if you can catch it and drink it
> you'll have good luck.

Nod

> Indications of progeny, beware
> teratogens and mountebanks.

The March

> Malefic planets bring disaster winds.
> Fortify your house, bar the doors, better
> not to have windows at all.

Moss House

> Luminaries in this sign bring riches,
> canned goods, winterwheat harvest and
> red berries.

Warp

> You will be nervous, you will have the
> shakes, you will shiver under fever
> blankets. If you persevere you will gain
> the world.

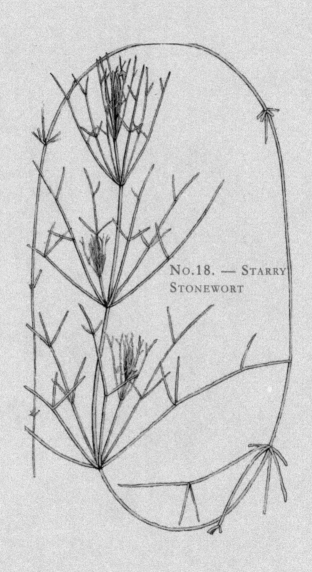

No.18. — Starry Stonewort

No.19. — TRAPDOOR
SNAIL

Trapdoor Snail

After the acidification of 2044 C.E.
there was still no fathoming the waters.
Cloudy life, algae, fading secchi discs,
fish scales hiding something
bottomless from us
deeper than the Foshay,
the Witch's Hat, or the Stepped Tower.

Out of that endless hole they came,
escaping the clarity that was death
for want of oxygen.
Regal, slimy, and glistening,
twelve yellow grubs on all their shells.

She was the only one who wanted
to discard the mother of pearl
and wrap her tongue into legs.

Change isn't hard in these times
but people touched her like knives,
knives, operettas, and brine in your eyes.

Until she wished her body
was made out of sea foam
and could cloud the waters again.

Walnut Twig Beetle

No one dies of thousand cankers disease,
no one but trees, my doctor said.

You're not a tree are you?
Not last time I checked but

I've been eating beetles since the crops died
and the basement with the preserves flooded

and the DNR stopped giving cash for clams
and more than my stomach went hollow.

They used to say black walnuts poisoned every
ground they touched
but at least they were edible.

What poisons the poisoners?

I can't walk to the clinic anymore,
my feet full of holes like cigarette burns,
my knees like joinery waiting for joints,

my face taking comfort
pressed against the cool of the heavy
walnut dining table

while a hole riddles my heart.

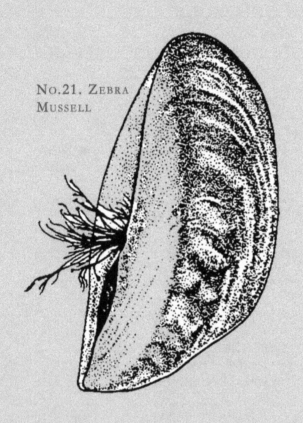

No.21. Zebra Mussell

Zebra Mussel

This twisting pass from delta downwards holds the little purses. Invasive, clasped to their cliff-sides, anchored with byssal threads and fed by probing feet. I, their ragged bounty hunter, pocketing the mirrored shells.

A chum bucket of zebra mussels earns you an extra ration from the DNR.

The little hitchhikers come in from the polar seas, desperate for Minnesota's tepid new latitudes. I do my civic duty gathering bivalves for a job recommendation, an unemployment extension, even just a Sunday afternoon spent with finger long fry sunnies with emerging legs, loons that lost theirs some year along the way.

On my way home, two fishers with metal teeth grab a snapping turtle by its furred scruff like I might have my mean old cat before he dried up and blew away in the wind. *Look what we caught.* I slow to watch the weirdness and how when they crack off the shell, pearls fall from the crevice now shattered into a glistening two-shelled organism. *That isn't where they come from.*

I try to remember the way the world is supposed
to work

sputtering past basalt bluffs and shining rainbows
of nacre strings of dead lights, Cambrian, past a
dead raccoon pearls spilling out its guts sliding on
white ball bearings bad as a mid-spring oil
planing.

I skid into the dark and wonder what world I'm
entering and what hot hell I'm leaving behind,
thrilled at the thought of what's growing inside
me

I wrote these poems when I lived in Minnesota—is it that obvious?—where there are four impossibly dramatic seasons per year, with heatwaves in the summer replaced by thermometers reading -40 in the winter (Celsius or Fahrenheit! That's the number where it doesn't matter and they're both the same.) The state has huge swathes of rural areas with only a handful of what people would consider "larger" cities, with beautiful parks, libraries, and arts nonprofits. It also has some of the worst inequality in the country, the most segregation, and the most violent policing. It's where I started school a second time, dropped out of school a second time, got my first apartment, broke down, built up, got married, met my most beloved friends, where I made my first professional story sale. It's where nearly my entire adult life happened. It's full of prairies, birch forests, sandstone bluffs, night markets, brownstones, NIMBYism, and collectives. One of my goals was to spend one night camping in every single state park, I got nowhere close before I left.

But between writing these poems and publication, I left all of that. I drove across the country with my husband and two dogs to far northern California - think significantly closer to Oregon than San Francisco. There are no seasons, no nearby big cities. It's famous for being the filming location for the speeder scenes in return of the Jedi, a lot of Bigfoot sightings, America's original weed destination, and possibly sightings of Bigfoot smoking weed.

It was winter when we left, in a middle-aged van with no chains and no snow tires. So instead of taking the most direct route through the Rockies, we went south through bits of lots of states, then north through the whole longitude of California.

On the way, in between catching dog vomit in gas station coffee cups, I got to see landscapes that were absolutely unknown and delightful to me. I loved the mushroom-shaped rocks of . . . well . . . Mushroom Rock State Park and read The Fungi From Yuggoth while we picnicked there on the last cold day of our trip. Less lovable were the land oil rigs that seemed set up on every farm. I loved the Saguaro that went on for infinity in Arizona. I didn't love and was disgusted that Customs & Border Patrol can run random checkpoints one hundred miles or less from a border. But the things I hated were part of the landscape too. I loved the Salton Sea, which a small corner of me had been aching to see ever since I learned about it from Kate Jonez Ceremony of Flies, somewhere I never really thought I'd go. Abandoned houses, live birds, and a beach with more dead fish than grains of sand around California's largest lake. It was a disaster of early American terraforming. As much as I loved it, I'm sure my dog loved rolling in the stinky sand even more.

Everywhere I went, I saw books in these landscapes, or landscapes in these books. The same way I did when I wrote this collection of poems, except I also wanted to stress not just a sense of place, but a sense of time. Like any good multidimensional traveler, I wanted to address a sense of space and time.

The Salton Sea didn't exist until an accident in 1905 filled a dry basin. On the contrary, it's almost a lie to talk about the Minnesota prairie currently. Only 1% of the area's original prairie remains today. Some of the species touched on in this book have been in Minnesota less than the average person. Zebra mussels date to the 1980s, some are even more recent additions, and some are hundreds of years old.

One of the more famous examples of invasive species introduction in the world is Eugene Schieffelin, whose dream was to release every single bird species mentioned in Shakespeare in North America. Again, the line between literature and landscape seems to blur. In 1890-1891, he released a hundred starlings into Central Park. This is 50 years before the first use of the word "terraform" but it seems like that concept, or a gooier, proto-version has been on people's minds much earlier, as we outsourced it to other species.

There are a lot of reasons why I wanted to write poetry taking place in a near-future. I mean, not always - sometimes I want to write about far-flung distance futures, or period Gothics, but I especially feel like stories of the near future are most important. There's something vital about reading about a world where we might expect to see ourselves, not distant future generations, not people long dead. A climate change and ecological damage we will have to live with, not one foisted off 'til next century.

One of the best take-downs of "write what you know" comes from John Gardner's proposal to instead write the kind of story you want to read. So I wrote these poems, because I want to see other branches of speculative literature in the near future— not just sci-fi, but horror, or fairy tales. After all, the biggest ecological danger of invasive species is the monoculture they create.

Going back through this manuscript for me is a lot like taking a walk in Quaking Bog or at Minnehaha Falls, in Maplewood State Park or the north shore. Each poem is familiar even after all this time and space, a collection of all the reasons and experiences that influenced my writing.

For me, a typical walk through the woods is built through numerous repetitions. If there's time, I might try to find some loop or trail I haven't seen before, but if there isn't I'm content doing the same thing over and over again, because it's never actually the same. I get to examine my favorite plants, and see how they've changed. Right now that includes the tree with the huge, just impossibly big burl, a new corridor of tall Oregon grape I found the day before writing this, and a patch of three trillium—there's probably a numerology poem of its own to be found there.

For example, I knew I wanted to write about traveling performers, entertainment, and the classic 'flea circus.' I actually bought a gigantic digital suite of old vintage circus documents and learned a lot. Maybe this is old news to everyone but me, but I used to think flea circuses were a joke, kind of like sea monkeys—a barker would just have a box with fleas in it, and spin imaginary narratives about what they were doing. Turns out flea circuses actually had a lot going on—actual fleas doing high jumps and hauling around tiny chariots with their creepy, wee, overly strong bodies. In the end though, this is less about the animals and more about the brilliant and talented poets, musicians, and rennies I knew.

I remember walking along the river once with a girlfriend—the Mississippi, full of zebra mussels. We ran into two guys who had just caught a snapping turtle. This is of course pre-near future, the snapping turtles haven't yet mutated to have a proper scruff, and these guys were thankfully holding it correctly (on the sides of the shell) but they still had it terrifyingly close to their face and really wanted us to come check it out. We declined.

A lot of these poems are inspired by my grandparents' home. It was the kind of place where they had a fridge and a bait fridge. Being a small child looking for snacks and opening a bait fridge is, well, the stuff of horror stories. You could buy nightcrawlers at the gas station, but usually we'd dig for them. It was weird, as an adult, to learn that they weren't common to remote parts of Minnesota until sport and hobby fishing brought them there. It's where my family taught me to clean fish, which again, thankfully, haven't mutated to grow eyestalks yet.

I removed Buckthorn as part of a local prairie restoration group, introduced to me by one of my professors. We did it with gloves and shovels, but apparently at one point goats were introduced to try to eat them all. Luckily, the goats didn't become an even bigger problem that required an even bigger devourer. I'm not sure how long that scenario has ever chained itself, but I know in Australia, cane toads were introduced to eat some species of beetles. They did a horrible job eating the beetles, but became a frequent nuisance themselves. I've got to recommend the documentary Cane Toads: An Unnatural History here as some incredible nature film making and look at invasive species.

A couple of these poems are about folk tales and myths that different plants or animals brought to my mind. Trapdoor Snails pulls some of my favorite and most disconcerting images from The Little Mermaid. Others took little folk legends about the plants themselves and developed from there. Queen Anne's Lace, or Wild Carrot, is edible. It also has a tiny red dot in the middle of its flower. Supposedly, it is a piece of lace knitted by Queen Anne, who pricked herself on a needle and that dot is her blood. Of course, in my version I preferred to imagine not a tiny pinprick, but a huge gush a la The Shining.

Researching all of these organisms was a joy. Sometimes what originally struck me as simply an evocative name turned into a rabbit hole of online research and long searching walks in the woods. The incredible pollinator attraction of loosestrife and its millions of seeds. The beauty of the emerald ash borer. I hope these poems help other people see the beauty and weirdness that I think is under the surface of any living thing. Because each one of these plants and animals is beautiful and weird. They, almost paradoxically, make the case for protecting landscapes and endangered species and avoiding monoculture.

ACKNOWLEDGEMENTS

"Brittle Naiad" was published in Issue 3 (Summer 2019) of *Sycorax Journal*

IMAGE CREDITS

The majority of the images in this book are from public domain or open source publications. We are thankful to the following digital resources from which the images were adapted:

The Internet Archive
The Biodiversity Heritage Library
New York Botanical Garden, LuEsther T. Mertz Library
The Marine Biological Laboratory (MBL) and Woods Hole Oceanographic Institution (WHOI).
University of Illinois Urbana-Champaign Library
Smithsonian Libraries
USDA Department of Agriculture, Natural Resources Conservation Service
The British Library
University of California Libraries
UBC Library
University of Washington Freshwater and Marine Image Bank
Cornell University Library
NOAA, US Great Lakes Environmental Research Library

About the Author

Amelia Gorman lived in Minneapolis for fifteen years before moving to Eureka, California in 2018. She loves the tide pools, redwood forests, and kinetic sculptures of her new home but misses lakes, looking at snow with a hot drink in her hand, public transit, and Eat Street. You can read more of her poetry in *Liminality, Star*Line, Vastarien,* and other places. She also writes weird fiction, including stories in *She Walks in Shadows* from *Innsmouth Free Press* and *Nox Pareidolia* from *Nightscape Press.*

Find her online on twitter at @gorman_ghast and www.ameliagorman.com.

INTERSTELLAR FLIGHT PRESS

Interstellar Flight Press is an indie speculative publishing house. We feature innovative works from the best new writers in science fiction and fantasy. In the words of Ursula K. Le Guin, we need "writers who can see alternatives to how we live now, can see through our fear-stricken society and its obsessive technologies to other ways of being, and even imagine real grounds for hope."

Find us online at www.interstellarflightpress.com.